Bremen Travel Highlights

Best Attractions & Experiences

Jodi Holmes

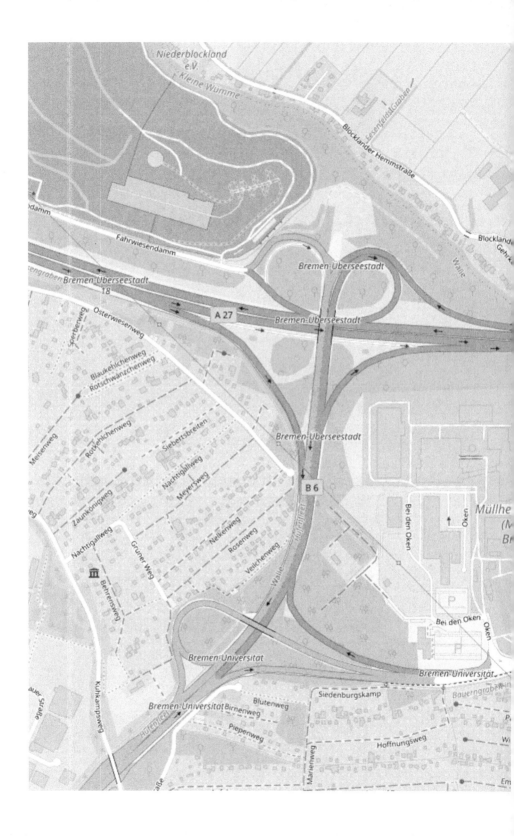

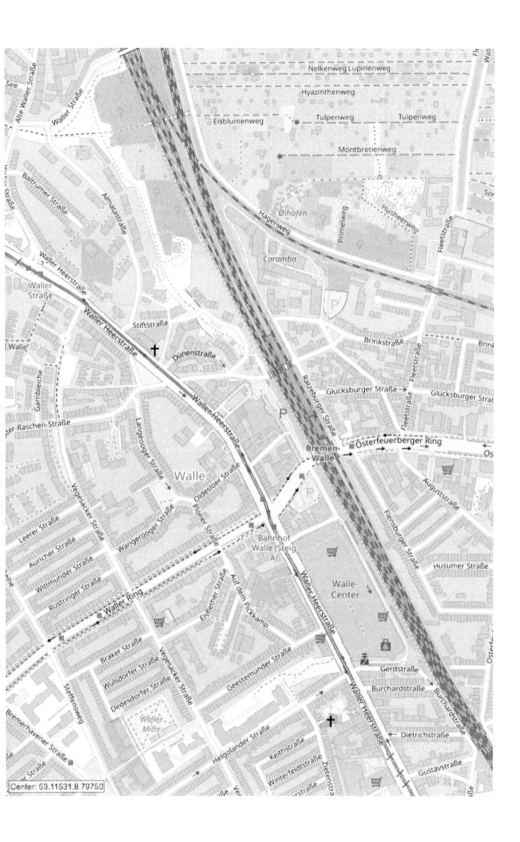

Contents

Welcome to Bremen

Visit the birthplace of the Brothers Grimm and take in the culture of the picturesque old-world city of Bremen in northern Germany, with its cobblestone streets, quaint shops and narrow canals. Marvel at the St. Peter's Cathedral, the Roland statue and historic buildings like the town hall. Bremen has remained a centre for commercial, economic and cultural life in Germany since the 11th century.

☐ 1. Town Musicians of Bremen

Address: 1 Schoppensteel, Bremen 28195, Germany

The Town Musicians of Bremen is a German fairy tale recorded by the brothers Jacob and Wilhelm Grimm in "Grimms' Fairy Tales" in 1819. You will see numerous references to the fable in Bremen. It tells the story of four aging farm animals that decide to flee their owners and set out on a journey to seek for better fortunes in the city of Bremen. The animals disguise themselves as musicians. After being discovered by a dog catcher, they are brought before a judge, who condemns them to exile from their homeland. The musicians make their appeal and eventually succeed in getting their sentence overturned.

□ 2. Schlachte Promenade

Address: 24 Schlachte, Bremen 28195, Germany

A walk along the Schlachte promenade in Bremen, just north of the River Weser, is a must for tourists to get a taste of local culture. Once one of the city's harbours, it is now packed with new and traditional restaurants, cafes and beer gardens. The bustling centre of this shopping area is home to traditional Schnoor.

□ 3. Schnoor Medieval Town

Address: 17 Schnoor, Bremen 28195, Germany
Web: http://www.schnoor-in-bremen.de/

The Schnoor is a neighbourhood in the medieval centre of the city of Bremen, and the part that has preserved a medieval character. The neighbourhood owes its name to old handicrafts associated with shipping. The alleys between the houses were often associated with occupations or objects: There was an area in which ropes and cables were produced and a neighboring area, where wire cable was manufactured. From this, comes another old nickname for the Schnoor – "The Alley of Ropes - Kabelgatt".

□ 4. Town Hall

Address: Am Markt 21, 28195 Bremen, Germany
Phone: +49 421 30 800 10
Web: http://www.rathaus-bremen.de/

The City Hall of Bremen (German: Bremisches Ratshaus) is the seat of the President of the Senate and Mayor of the Free Hanseatic City of Bremen. It is one of the most important examples of Brick Gothic and Weser Renaissance architecture in Europe. Since 1973, it has been a protected historical building. In July 2004, along with the Bremen Roland statue, the building was added to the list of UNESCO World Heritage Sites.

☐ 5. Glockenspiel House

The Carillon, a musical instrument made up of at least 23 cast bronze bells, sits atop the Glockenspiel House, Bremen. The bells are from Germany's Royal Meissen Porcelain Factory and were made between 1738 and 1999. When it was built in 1913, the tower was simply a clock tower for a local real estate company called Celler & Schüle. In 2004 it became a museum dedicated to seafarers and aviators.

☐ 6. Saint Peter's Cathedral

Web: http://www.stpetridom.de/

St. Peter's Cathedral is in the heart of old Bremen and is a mixture of styles: the nave and choir in Gothic style and the interior in Byzantine style. The Cathedral of St. Peter is an enormous Protestant Church located in the city's Altstadt. Its tall spires can be seen from afar. Due to its unusual leaning posture, the cathedral has been nicknamed "the drunken sailor". The current building was built during 1360-1520 years after the northern tower started crumbling.

☐ 7. Science Center

Address: Wiener Str. 1a, 28359 Bremen, Germany

Phone: +49 421 33460

Email: info@universum-bremen.de

Web: https://universum-bremen.de/

The Universum Bremen is a science museum in Bremen, which is nationally and internationally renowned for its exhibits on technology, media, communications, health, nature and society. More than 300 motion picture scenes are shown, including about 10 world-exclusive special effects. Visitors are encouraged to touch most of the 250 exhibits during their visit.

☐ 8. Die Glocke Concert Hall

Web: http://www.glocke.de/

Die Glocke is a concert hall in the centre of Bremen. Standing on the site of a building from the Middle Ages, it was designed by Walter Görig and completed in 1928. Its elegant Art Deco design and excellent acoustics have been praised by a number of artists including Herbert von Karajan.

□ 9. Bleikeller

Address: 1 Am Dom, Bremen 28195, Germany

The Bleikeller, in Bremen, is a historic underground beer cellar dating back to the early 13th century.

☐ 10. Wasserkunst Fountain

Wasserkunst, Bremen is a large hammer-worked fountain (wasserkunst) in Bremen. It is situated by the central market square (Marktplatz). Every day the fountain runs for at least a few minutes. It consists of two towers with multiple water jets.

□ 11. Skulpturengarten

Address: 3 Am Markt, Bremen 28195, Germany

The Skulpturengarten, Bremen is the sculpture garden of the Kunsthalle Bremen. It is an art museum with a focus on modern and contemporary works of art. The offerings include international as well as German creations by many famous artists. The museum has part of its collection in storage which can be explored on the official website.

□ 12. Paula Modersohn-Becker Museum

Address: Böttcherstraße 6–10, 28195 Bremen, Germany

Phone: +49 421 338 82 22

Email: info@pmbm.de

The Paula Modersohn-Becker Museum in Bremen is devoted to preserving the legacy of Paula Modersohn-Becker's fascinating life and work. This private museum showcases key works from all of her different creative periods. Her best-known painting, "I painted myself" (1908), is at the core of the collection. The museum features her paintings, graphics, drawings, and personal belongings including letters, diaries, gowns, and more.

□ 13. Art Hall Bremen

Address: Am Wall 207, 28195 Bremen, Germany
Phone: +49 421 32908 0
Email: office@kunsthalle-bremen.de
Web: https://www.kunsthalle-bremen.de/

Art from the 19th century to the present is displayed in this museum in the heart of Bremen, along with one-of-a-kind art installations. This building, which was constructed in 1849, has been expanded repeatedly over the years, most notably in 2002 and 2011. The 11 galleries in this striking piece of architecture include a permanent collection that includes works by Picasso and Salvador Dalí, as well as a large collection of paintings by Bremen artists from the 16th through 19th century.

□ 14. Weserburg Museum of Modern Art

Email: info@weserburg.de
Web: http://www.weserburg.de/

Overlooking the River Weser, the Weserburg is a museum of modern art in Bremen. Located in a former industrial warehouse of 1947, it opened in 1991 and consists of 5 architects' studios and a small auditorium. The museum is designed to showcase contemporary works of art by various artists, Oldenburg being a proponent of the museum's new approach to collecting art. Today, the museum houses exhibitions of works by international artists on invitation from its permanent collection committee.

□ 15. Wilhelm Wagenfeld House

Web: http://www.wwh-bremen.de/

The Wilhelm Wagenfeld House is a design museum and exhibition centre in Bremen. Completed in the neoclassical style in 1828, the building now carries the name of Bremen-born Wilhelm Wagenfeld, a major contributor to the 20th-century design of household objects. In addition to a collection of Wagenfeld's creations, the building hosts temporary design exhibitions. It is located in Bremen's Old Market.

□ 16. Bremen Roland Statue

Address: 1 Am Markt, Bremen 28195, Germany

In the market square of Bremen, stands a statue made of red sandstone. In 1404, as a sign of the city-state's power and wealth as a member of the Hanseatic League, the statue was erected. The statue is known as Roland and shows Roland – or more accurately his likeness – with his legendary sword pointing skyward and with an unsheathed sword at his side. The larger than life statue also features symbols and descriptions of his history and association with the city-state, including that he is handling an Imperial eagle.

□ 17. Ethnological Museum Bremen

Address: Bahnhofsplatz 13, 28195 Bremen, Germany
Phone: +49 421 160380
Email: office@uebersee-museum.de

Web: http://www.uebersee-museum.de/

The Museum is located in an historic monument, the old building of the Senate (1860-1861), built in Italian Villa Style. With its almost 1000 objects, displays about 50 countries and their cultures, besides animals and plants living in tropical regions. The exhibits came from many expeditions (Ritter expedition to New Guinea, Triang & Schück expedition to Cameroon), trade contacts (cocoa beans from India), mission stations (including former mission station Yal in Lower Saxony).

☐ 18. Am Wall Windmill

The tall and narrow Am Wall Windmill, or "Am-Wallmuehle" as it is called locally, is an imposing building on the hill overlooking Bremen's inner harbor. Its clock tower rises 66 meters (217 feet) above the surrounding rooftops. Opened in 1898, it is one of the last of the many windmills that once dotted northern Germany. Today it serves as a restaurant and shopping area.

☐ 19. Metropol Theater Bremen

Address: 6 Grünenweg, Bremen 28195, Germany
Web: https://metropol-theater-bremen.de/

The Metropol Theater Bremen is a renowned theatre in the city of Bremen that has been providing entertainment since 1926. With its modern, bold style this theatre attracts a diverse audience each season. In the heart of the German city it would be hard to pass by this beautiful building without noticing. The bold colors from the outside provide a pop of color among the buildings along the street. Unique architecture sets it apart from others around it.

□ 20. Ludwig Roselius Museum

The Ludwig Roselius Museum, Bremen is a museum of international importance for the history of coffee. In the museum's exhibition area of almost 1,500 square meters, large numbers of historical objects from the private culture collection of the F.A.S. Group are shown. Ludwig Roselius, the inventor of decaffeinated coffee and founder of the mercantile company Kaffee HAG, bought the building in 1902.

☐ 21. Martinikirche

The Martinikirche, Bremen was originally constructed in the 12th century. This church has undergone major renovations since then, including the construction of the south tower in the late 15th century. Located adjacent to its sister church, Jacobikirche, both churches are popular tourist destinations known for their incredible stained glass windows.

☐ 22. Gerhard Marcks House

Web: http://www.marcks.de/

The Museum is located in a building designed by the architect Hans Schwippert, which was constructed in 1958 to house the Chamber of Commerce. The building was designed with a sober facade of brick and glass, but Marcks added a sculptural relief, signed by him and mounted on the eastern wall on Rindermarkt. Its graphic forms are reminiscent of his Black Sun from 1927. Schwippert's building underwent various conversions during the years, including most recently to house the museum and named after its founding patron.

□ 23. Hafenmuseum Speicher XI

Phone: +49 421 3038279
Web: https://www.hafenmuseum-speicherelf.de/

The Hafenmuseum Speicher XI is located in the Speicherstadt, an old warehouse district of Bremen which was constructed as a commercial harbor site after the year 1830. Discover the 120-year history of Bremen's harbour inside this historical cotton warehouse. Delve into the history of the development of the area from overseas harbour to a modern, urban neighbourhood.

☐ 24. Fallturm (Gravitational Tower)

Address: 2 Am Fallturm, Bremen 28359, Germany

The Fallturm Bremen is a gravitational tower at the Center of Applied Space Technology and Microgravity (Zentrum für angewandte Weltraumforschung und Mikrogravitation, ZAWM) at the University of Bremen. It was built between 1988 and 1990, and includes a 122-metre-high drop tube, in which weightlessness can be produced for 4.74 seconds. The entire tower, formed out of a reinforced concrete shank, is 146 metres high.

☐ 25. Mühle Oberneuland (Windmill)

The Oberneulander Mühle is a Dutch-style windmill in the district of Oberneuland. The mill was built in the 17th century and has been a listed building since 1953. The mill has been open to the public as a branch of the Bremen State Museum for Art and Cultural History since 1972. In addition to the mill technology, the permanent exhibition From Grain to Bread can be visited. The mill is fully operational as well.

□ 26. Robinson Crusoe House

Ludwig Roselius was a coffee merchant in Bremen. He admired the pioneering spirit of Daniel Defoe's fictional hero Robinson Crusoe. In the early 20th century, Roselius built a house in Bremen that combined elements of an English country house and a tropical island hut to showcase his product. The family lived in the house until World War II, when it became a museum with Roselius's collection of antiquities.

□ 27. Focke's Wind Tunnel

The Focke Wind Tunnel, in Bremen, is a fully operational wind tunnel. It was built by Henrich Focke, an aviation pioneer who co-founded Focke-Wulf and worked with a team to design a fully-controllable helicopter for practical use in aerial warfare. The laboratory in the city of Bremen, was finished by 1960 and remained in the Focke family until 2004.

□ 28. Schnoor

Address: 20 Schnoor, Bremen 28195, Germany

The Schnoor ("rope/cable neighbourhood") is a neighbourhood in the old town of Bremen. Its name derives from the 15th century when rope makers and wire drawers worked here. It is one of the few parts of Bremen's inner city area that was not turned into a war-ruin in the last World War. Today, nearly all houses are rebuilt or restored to their former glory. Bollards in this area are painted red topped by white spheres, recalling the shape of soap bubbles.

□ 29. Gymnasium Leibnizplatz & Realschule

Leibnizplatz & Realschule, Bremen is the perfect location for field trips, team building exercises, or off-site meetings. This facility offers modern classrooms, including laptop desks, projectors that display content on screens, and an audio/visual system. It also offers spacious locker rooms for both men and women. The natural light makes this space feel warm and welcoming.

□ 30. Cinema im Ostertor

Phone: +49 421 700 914
Web: http://www.cinema-ostertor.de/

Located in Bremen on the banks of the Weser river on Gröpelingerstraße 21. Cinema im Ostertor has shown film continuously since 1919. It has presented all types of cinema including newsreels, cartoons, short films, Hollywood features and German classics. During WWII it remained open and showed Nazi propaganda films. After the war it remained a respectable cinema showing the latest releases during the 1950s and 60s under its manager Kurt Harmsen.

□ 31. Schulschiff Deutschland (Students' Ship)

Web: https://schulschiff-deutschland.de/

The Schulschiff Deutschland (Students' Ship Germany) is a German full-rigged sail training ship, maintained as a historical monument and museum ship. She was employed as a school ship for the merchant marine beginning in 1927. The ship is moored at Vegesack, in the Federal State of Bremen. Since the name Deutschland was at the time of its construction already assigned to an unbuilt naval warship, its official name has since been simplified to Schulschiff Deutschland.

☐ 32. Anti-Colonialism Memorial

Address: Hermann-Böse-Straße, Bremen 28209, Germany

The Antikolonialdenkmal in Bremen is a memorial that commemorates the victims of slavery. It was designed by the artist Mark-Anthony Turnage. It is made from concrete, steel, brass, and aluminium, and the sculpture depicts men and women in chains, marching towards freedom. The monument was constructed to honor the victims of the Scramble for Africa and to condemn colonialism as an instrument of imperialism.

□ 33. Stadtwaage

The Stadtwaage, Bremen is located at No. 13 Langenstraße in the city center. The municipal weighing scales were built in 1445 and it is believed to be Germany's oldest hospital for weighing goods. Town merchants could bring their goods to the Stadtwaage to be weighed, which avoided the need for ships or carriages to travel to Bremerhaven or Bremen.

☐ 34. Heineken House

The Heineken House is a historic building with exceptional cultural heritage in Bremen. The house was built in the 18th century with its exterior style of an old townhouse, and has several rooms decorated with medieval paintings and a painted wooden ceiling.

☐ 35. Focke Museum of History & Art

Address: 240 Schwachhauser Heerstraße, Bremen 28213, Germany

The Focke Museum is the museum of history and art in Bremen. it was formed in 1924 by the merger of two museums, an Industrial and Commerce Museum and a previous Historical Museum. It officially opened on 23 November 1925. Its founder was Johann Focke (German aviation pioneer) who donated his collection of aerial photographs, original components of aircraft and World War I memorabilia. Over time it has grown to include over 11 million historical objects dating back to the beginnings of humankind.

☐ 36. Theater am Goetheplatz

The Theater am Goetheplatz, also known as the "Goethetheater", is the main theatre of the city of Bremen. Built between 1911 and 1913 in the Neoclassical style, it is located in the cultural district to the east of Bremen's old town. After reconstruction following Second World War damage, which included adding a third storey, it was extensively modernised in 2005.

☐ 37. Warehouse XI Port City

Nestled in a stylish portside city on the Weser river is a place where over 100 companies from around the world have come to do business. Most of them are international companies. The Warehouse XI, Bremen, offers a distinctive working environment for each company that rents space here - whether it be a car tyre manufacturer from South Africa, a software developer from Great Britain or a production line from Sweden.

☐ 38. Schweizerhaus

Address: 2 Bürgerpark, Bremen 28209, Germany

The Schweizerhaus is a 500 year old, traditional German restaurant. It is located right in the historical center of Bremen. In this restaurant, everything revolves around the famous Schnitzel and other dishes from Germany, prepared with fresh ingredients from the vicinity. With indoor and outdoor seating, the Schweizerhaus offers a wide variety of German beers and German food. Its beer garden has an open fire in winter where guests can get warm while enjoying beers, schnapps, spiced wine, and other drinks.

□ 39. Suding & Soeken Building

The Suding & Soeken building at No. 28 Langenstraße in Bremen is a merchant house noted for its projecting Renaissance bay window and its two-tiered Baroque stairway ascending from the hallway. The symmetrical facade, popular in northern Germany during the 16th century, consists of two to four 17th-century gable-end bays. In one of these bays, there is a projection in which there was once a Renaissance bay window but which now contains a Baroque entrance portal.

☐ 40. St Petrus House (Atlantic Grand Hotel)

Built in 1927 by Ludwig Roselius, the owner of the coffee company, the Petrus House is an historic building located in Bremen. At the time it was built, his coffee company was one of the three largest in Germany. The term "petrus" is Latin for stone, which was used to refer to the building's entrance portal. It also features patios and arcades that are classic structures within North-German Gothic architecture. Today it houses the Atlantic Grand Hotel Bremen Böttcherstraße.

☐ 41. St Catherine's Monastery

St Catherine's Monastery in Bremen, was founded in 1253 by the Dominicans. Today traces of its existence remain in the area of the Katharinenstraße and Katharinenklosterhof in the old town. During the Thirty Years' War (1618-1648) parts of it were destroyed.

☐ 42. Spitzen Gebel

The Spitzen Gebel ("pointed steeple") is a historic building in the center of Bremen. It is located at No. 1, Hinter dem Schütting. A gable-ended timber-framed building from 1420 with a late Gothic hall house from 1590, it is partially enclosed by a still-extant pointed timber-framed bell tower from 1610. It has been owned by the city of sister town Bremen since 1927 and has been a listed building since 1973 due to its Renaissance architecture.

□ 43. Rathscafé (Deutsches Haus)

Deutsches Haus is a listed building on the market place in Bremen. Built during 1887–1888 by Carl Raschdorff, the establishment was initially called Café Reimers, with its name being derived from the land owner Carl Reimers senior. The Café was later renamed Rathscafé. Finally it became Deutsches Haus when in 1977, before the city regained its historical city-state status, it hosted the function of an embassy of West Germany in GDR times.

□ 44. Raths-Apotheke Pharmacy

The Raths-Apotheke is a listed building on the Market Square in Bremen. The ground floor of the arcaded building from the 1840s was converted to an apothecary's shop in 1834. The name of this pharmacist's shop, which is still open today, alludes to the building's former function as a university library. Its preserved name over the entryway is decorated with the bust of Minerva. After suffering war damage, the rebuilding of 1958 replaced two domes at either end of the building with two gables in the Neobaroque style.

□ 45. Main Post Office Building

The building was designed by architect Georg Frentzen (1822-1906), who started with the completion of the basilica St. Petri, which is situated at one end of Domshof square. The Main Post Office Building is part of the ensemble of listed buildings on Domsheide square, among them are St. Petri church, St. Andreas church (parts of the city hall), the city hall itself, and the Bremen Market House.

☐ 46. Landherrnamt Building

The Landherrnamt, meaning "Landed Gentry Office" in German, is a building located in the Schnoor district of Bremen. Designed by Alexander Schröder and built between 1854 and 1856, it is a Bremen landmark and is used as a location for photoshoots and film, notably as the "Das Landgericht", or state court, in the 2004 movie adaptation of John Irving's novel The World According to Garp.

☐ 47. House of the Seven Lazy Brothers

The House of the Seven Lazy Brothers has been so named for over 300 years and is one of Bremen's most famous houses. Its seven stories rise above a bay-like roof and each story is higher than the preceding room. The Böttcherstraße façade was designed by architect Alfred Runge and represents a steep flight of stairs, interrupted by numerous bow windows capped with figures from the Old Testament. The figures present an unusual mix from Old Testament figures such as Moses or King

David to figures from Ancient Greece or Rome, such as Hercules or Minerva.

□ 48. Haus der Stadtsparkasse

The Haus der Stadtsparkasse is a Rococo landmark on the 'Marktplatz' in Bremen. It was completed in the 1950s combining the historic front gable from another site with the more recent architecture of the remainder of the building.

□ 49. Deutsche Bank Building

The building was erected by the local Deutsche Bank in a historicist style and was, with a floor space of almost 20,000m^2 at the time, one of the largest office buildings north of the Alps. The building is seen as a monument to the economic success of Bremen during this time. Early on, it housed not only the local branch of Deutsche Bank itself but also its subsidiaries and other banks from outside Bremen. From 1892 to 1923, this was Germany's national bank.

□ 50. Bremen Main Post Office Building

The building was erected on the site of a former big brick yard as the first purpose-built post office for Bremen. Construction began in 1898, and was completed by 1905 after some redesigning following criticism from the postal service inspectors. Its concave facade on Domsheide with five windows on each side is characteristic of Neo-Renaissance architecture. It has a U-shaped floor plan with a large yard surrounding it. The front entrance is preceded by a portico with four Ionic columns.

☐ 51. Bremen Cotton Exchange

In 1872, a cotton exchange was opened in Bremen. In 1902, the association acquired a piece of land next to the town hall and commissioned well-known local architect Johann Poppe to build a Neo-Renaissance building there. The Bremen Cotton Exchange features a glass atrium that reaches up to the rooftop. The buildings tallest point is 34 meters high and made out of colorfully painted ironwork.

☐ 52. Spuckstein-Gesche Gottfried Monument

Address: 8 Domshof, Bremen 28195, Germany

An exceptional German porcelain figure by Gesche Gottfried is the Spuckstein national monument in Bremen. Behind this statue is a story of a man who survived the bubonic plague. He was put on display as a curiosity and became a symbol of hope and recovery at a time when 25% of Germany's population had been wiped out. He was then popularized as a good luck figure for many years before being placed at the current location.

□ 53. Wätjens Park

Picture yourself strolling through the Wätjens Park, Bremen, in the vicinity of the Nord-Ostsee-Kanal. This green space is popular with locals and visitors alike. Hills covered with junipers and chestnut trees fill the background while majestic chestnut trees claim the foreground. Children will find plenty of room for running around while parents can relax in one of the many benches along this lovely 4 km long park.

☐ 54. Villa Steinbrügge

Villa Steinbrügge, a hotel in Bremen offers a clinical wellness experience combining art and science for a holistic approach to health and beauty. Over the past six years Dr. Silke Brandenburg has been working with leading international scientists from Harvard Medical School and beyond, conducting scientific trials exploring the effects of certain groups of natural materials on human cell lines, biochemical patterns and other parameters at Hamburg University. The resultant synergies have been translated into an effective wellness formula available for guests seeking to achieve a specific objective.

☐ 55. Villa Korff

Villa Korff is a Boutique Villa, located in the picturesque city of Bremen. This stunning property boasts breathtaking views across the city and river towards the North Sea. Surrounded by magnificent gardens, the villa offers every imaginable amenity, making it the perfect location for an unforgettable wedding or honeymoon.

☐ 56. Turnhalle Arena

Since the First World War, Turnhalle has been a venue for entertainment as well as a place of learning. In fact, it is a venue where you can enjoy both, as it is a combination of a theater and a sports arena. It is also an indoor circus arena.

☐ 57. Torhäuschen House

Address: 211 Am Staatsarchiv, Bremen 28195, Germany

The Torhäuschen, Bremen is a decorative half-timbered house. Its one of the landmarks or stops along the UNESCO World Heritage Site, which is the old town center of Bremen – known as Böttcherstraße. The building was established there around 1790 and is now under ownership by a private individual, but still contains a café and souvenir shop.

☐ 58. Tabakbörse Tobacco Marketplace

The Tabakbörse, Bremen is an auction house and market located in Bremen, and specializing in antique and collectible tobacco and smoking accessories. The auction house has been in operation since 1870 and the auction catalog is filled with all kinds of interesting and fascinating smoking-related antiques that range from pipes to tobacco scales and beyond. Each item has its own historical story, but once the auction ends these items will be packed up and shipped.

☐ 59. Steinernes Kreuz

> ***Address:*** 12 Beim Steinernen Kreuz, Bremen 28203, Germany

The Steinernes Kreuz ("Stone Cross"), also called the Bremen Cross, is a large 13th-century sculpted stone block with a cross in a circular frame in the chapel of the Cathedral of the Prince-Archbishopric of Bremen. The cross itself was carved from a single piece of granite. Its construction may have been started by William II, Count of Bremen-Verden, who died in 1260/1267, but it is believed that it was not completed before 1290.

☐ 60. St. Jakobus-Packhaus Refugee Site

The St. Jakobus-Packhaus is a nonprofit organization that helps refugees integrate into communities. It provides free German classes for 1-2 years and support services. In 1878, a priest came up with the idea for a new kind of institution. It would be a place where young men from far away places could spend a few weeks in Bremen learning to speak German and finding work. The St. Jakobus-Packhaus is still going strong today providing help to people from all over the world.

☐ 61. Rathaus Hemelingen

The Rathaus Hemelingen is the former town hall in Hemelingen District, Bremen. A restaurant is located here since 2013.

☐ 62. Oelzweig-Haus Mansion

Address: 8 Kurfürstenallee, Bremen 28211, Germany

Built in 1905 and designed by the famous German architect and designer, Otto Apel, this 10 room mansion is known as Oelzweig-Haus. The Italian-style architecture and abundant use of limestone that defines this mansion's aesthetics makes it one of the most beautiful mansions in Germany. The mansion combines features such as elaborate murals, stained glass windows, statues and other ornate items made from marble and stone.

☐ 63. Nikolaikirche Oslebshausen

Address: 3 Ritterhuder Heerstraße, Bremen 28239, Germany

The Nikolaikirche Oslebshausen in Bremen is a great example

of a Romanesque architecture. Behind the church there is a memorial stone in honor of Dietrich Bonhoeffer. Today's bell dates from 1929. Its bigger sister had to be given up during the Second World War

☐ 64. Kulturhaus Walle

The Kulturhaus Walle is a cultural centre in Bremen. Made

up of two buildings, opposite each other on either side of Fuldastrasse, the centre combines cinemas, museums, concert halls, art exhibitions and more into one exciting place to visit.

□ 65. Knoops Park

Address: Bremen 28759, Germany

The Knoops Park is the first city park in the highest building of Bremen. Situated at the top of a new residential building it features a beer garden integrated into the concept of the roof terrace of which you will enjoy an outstanding panoramic view over Bremen's old town, the river Weser and more than 40 neighboring cities.

□ 66. Horner Kirche

The Horner Church, built in Bremen by the architect collective Gerkan, Marg and Partners (GMP), was nominated for the German Award for Architecture 2008. It is one of the most recent additions to the city. The church forms a new urban quarter on the edge of the medieval old town. The highest point is reached by an exciting staircase with transparent steps which seems to be suspended in the air. The roof structure with its spectacular form of perforated concrete shell resembles a giant bird's nest that swoops down to shelter the church beneath it.

Picture Credits

Schlachte Promenade: Jürgen Howaldt (CC BY-SA 2.0 de)

Town Hall: Zairon (CC0)

Glockenspiel House: Xocolatl (PD)

Saint Peter's Cathedral: Ulamm (CC BY-SA 3.0)

Science Center: Matthias Süßen (CC BY-SA 3.0)

Die Glocke Concert Hall: W. Bulach (CC BY-SA 4.0)

Bleikeller: Rami Tarawneh (CC BY-SA 2.5)

Wasserkunst Fountain: Matthias Süßen (CC BY-SA 3.0)

Skulpturengarten: Ulamm (CC BY-SA 3.0)

Paula Modersohn-Becker Museum: Kunstsammlungen Böttcherstraße (CC BY 2.5)

Art Hall Bremen: Verograph (CC BY-SA 3.0)

Weserburg Museum of Modern Art: Wynyard (CC BY-SA 3.0)

Wilhelm Wagenfeld House: Jürgen Howaldt (CC BY-SA 2.0 de)

Bremen Roland Statue: Ziko (CC BY-SA 3.0)

Ethnological Museum Bremen: Jürgen Howaldt (CC BY-SA 2.0 de)

Am Wall Windmill: Patrice (CC BY-SA 4.0)

Metropol Theater Bremen: (Christian) Jason Peper Trublu (CC BY-SA 2.5)

Ludwig Roselius Museum: Godewind (CC BY-SA 4.0)

Martinikirche: Jürgen Howaldt (CC BY-SA 2.0 de)

Gerhard Marcks House: Jürgen Howaldt (CC BY-SA 2.0 de)

Hafenmuseum Speicher XI: Romwriter (CC-BY-SA-3.0)

Fallturm (Gravitational Tower): Bin Im Garten (CC BY-SA 3.0)

Mühle Oberneuland (Windmill): Jürgen Howaldt (CC BY-SA 2.0 de)

Robinson Crusoe House: Jürgen Howaldt (CC BY-SA 2.0 de)

Focke's Wind Tunnel: Dr. Ing. Kai Steffen (CC-BY-SA-3.0)

Schnoor: Bahnfrend (CC BY-SA 4.0)

Gymnasium Leibnizplatz & Realschule: Jürgen Howaldt (CC BY-SA 2.0 de)

Cinema im Ostertor: Till F. Teenck (CC BY-SA 3.0)

Schulschiff Deutschland (Students' Ship): Cayambe (CC BY-SA 3.0)

Anti-Colonialism Memorial: Matthias Süßen (CC BY-SA 3.0)

Stadtwaage: Xocolatl (PD)

Heineken House: Jürgen Howaldt (CC BY-SA 2.0 de)

Focke Museum of History & Art: Jürgen Howaldt (CC BY-SA 2.0 de)

Theater am Goetheplatz: Florean Fortescue (CC BY-SA 3.0)

Warehouse XI Port City: Garitzko (PD)

Schweizerhaus: Till F. Teenck (CC BY-SA 3.0)

Suding & Soeken Building: Jürgen Howaldt (CC BY-SA 3.0 de)

St Petrus House (Atlantic Grand Hotel): Godewind (CC BY-SA 3.0)

Spitzen Gebel: Jürgen Howaldt (CC BY-SA 3.0 de)

Rathscafé (Deutsches Haus): Jürgen Howaldt (CC BY-SA 2.0 de)

Raths-Apotheke Pharmacy: Jürgen Howaldt (CC BY-SA 2.0 de)

Main Post Office Building: Rami Tarawneh (CC BY-SA 2.5)

Landherrnamt Building: Jocian (CC BY-SA 3.0)

House of the Seven Lazy Brothers: Jürgen Howaldt (CC BY-SA 2.0 de)

Haus der Stadtsparkasse: Jürgen Howaldt (CC BY-SA 2.0 de)

Deutsche Bank Building: Florean Fortescue (CC BY-SA 3.0)

Bremen Main Post Office Building: Rami Tarawneh (CC BY-SA 2.5)

Bremen Cotton Exchange: Jürgen Howaldt (CC BY-SA 2.0 de)

Spuckstein-Gesche Gottfried Monument: Jürgen Howaldt (CC BY-SA 2.0 de)

Wätjens Park: Quarz (CC BY-SA 3.0)

Villa Steinbrügge: Xenonx3 (CC0)

Villa Korff: Uwitte (CC BY-SA 3.0)

Turnhalle Arena: Hawei (CC BY-SA 4.0)

Tabakbörse Tobacco Marketplace: Matthias Süßen (CC BY-SA 3.0)

Steinernes Kreuz: Jürgen Howaldt (CC BY-SA 2.0 de)

Printed in Great Britain
by Amazon

80710936R00041